Third Eye Open

A soulful expression of prose poetry.

Marcus Wooten

BookLeaf Publishing
India | USA | UK

AF518995

Made with ❤ on the BookLeaf Publishing Platform
www.bookleafpub.in
www.bookleafpub.com

Dedication

To the quiet voices that stir within us, the echoes of experience, and the unwavering search for meaning. May this book offer solace and connection on your own soulful journey. Dedicated to the seekers, the feelers, the dreamers. May this prose illuminate the beauty and complexity of the human spirit, and may it offer a gentle hand on your path.

Preface

Welcome, kindred spirit, to a space where the echoes of the ancestors resonate in the rhythm of verse. Within these pages lies not just ink on paper, but the beating heart of a heritage – a soulful exploration of the Black experience rendered in a language that seeks to both embrace and transcend.

My aim is not simply to recount, but to reimagine. To offer a fresh lens through which to view the complexities of identity, the enduring legacy of our past, and the urgent conversations of our present. These poems grapple with the weight of history, the beauty of our cultural tapestry, the nuances of love and loss within our communities, and the unwavering quest for liberation in its myriad forms.

Acknowledgements

To my cherished family and dear friends, your voices and conversations sparked the very essence of these words. Thank you for the fire you ignited within me.

And to the three extraordinary women who nurtured this flame: my beloved mother, Viola Wooten; my guiding auntie, Asya Al-Aleem; and my steadfast girlfriend, Michelle Curts. Your constant encouragement and gentle prodding have given these words their wings. From the depths of my heart, thank you. I love you all deeply.

A Silent Narrative.

The one-legged woman, her silver hair a halo against the worn fabric of the bus seat, wheels herself aboard. Her calloused hands, strong as forged steel, grip the roll bars with a fierce determination, a silent battle against the unyielding metal. The bus beeps, an impatient sigh before the ramp extends, a Shanghai trapdoor opening to accept her slow progress. Slightly overweight, her arms betray a hidden strength, while thick glasses magnify eyes that hold a hint of perpetual seasickness, as if the world itself tilts precariously.

A whisper of a story forms unbidden: a medic tent under a relentless sun, the precise movements of her hands stitching a torn limb, offering a word of solace, then the blinding flash, the earth-shattering roar, a backpack's cruel payload stealing limbs and lives in an instant. Or perhaps a different path, a stumble into the abyss of inebriation, a moment of blurred vision, the sudden, brutal intrusion of headlights into darkness, a blink and then...absence.

Now, she navigates a two-legged world on a manual wheelchair, plastic bags – makeshift pockets filled with the meager treasures of a dollar store – rustling around her. Silver-haired lady, the lines etched on your face speak of dreams that shattered like glass, of choices that haunt the quiet hours. I sense the constant pressure of a world built for others, the hurried pace, the subtle manipulations of a system that profits from your loss. I see the impatient glances, the unempathetic rush of souls brushing past.

I feel the small indignities: the jarring halt as your wheels catch on a door jam, the strain of opening a heavy door while others politely avert their gaze. Living, once effortless, has become a wearying chore. One-legged, silver-haired lady in your wheelchair, do their eyes truly see the weight of your journey, the quiet sorrow that shadows your silver hair? Or am I alone in witnessing the story etched in the lines of your face, the silent testament to a life irrevocably altered?

What is Poetry?

Poetry, what is it? Could it be nouns, verbs, pronouns, objectives, and conjunctions that connects and creates a picture of
colorful bliss that communicates a beautiful tragedy or an ugly dream? It could be a graceful hummingbird that siphons
the sweet nectar of a Calla Lily bloom so vibrant and striking with the sun being its only match. Poetry, graceful and
powerful as a mother nurses life into her seed; mother earth and her child.

Could poetry be visions of burnt and rotting corpses scattered across war torn lands being devoured by vultures and
poisoning the third eye creating a stain on the consciousness, or could it be the way a women walks, the sway of her hips
as waves in the ocean rocking in its own harmony, so elegantly and enticing holding my attention as my head

sways back
and forth in matching the rhythm of the ocean of her
hips.

Poetry, when eyes meet and the explosion of imagination
with sparkles of ecstasy and lust that warms the blood.
One
voice of a thousand hearts communicating the one
thought of connection of love and passion. A scream
inside of the
mind, voices of pain and confusion with instructions to
self harm; voices never ending, the murmuring of a
beaten
consciousness.

Poetry, where language and soul unite, a delicate dance
of giving and receiving. Words, like lovers, embrace,
birthing
images from the womb of thought. Poetry paints
emotions, breathes life into the unseen. What form dose
poetry take for
you?

Table and Tea.

May I offer you tea, and a moment at this table? Let our voices weave a tapestry of rhythms and communication touching
each other souls with curiosity in searching for a connection. Let us drink the warm libation of wonder and amazement to
become intoxicated with anticipation and pleasure to explore the depths of our spirits.

The tea we share warms and soothes the dark places of my essence, as you warm my mind with your presence, the
words we exchange activates a flow of energy that felt between us. "Another cup?" "No thank you" I'm as heated as a hot
air balloon that floats amongst the clouds riding the currents of air in slow motion, absorbing the essence of your being.

This table we share, looking into each others windows

we see souls that yearns to be embraced, experiencing a
moment
of unity where nothing exist but each other and our table
where we exist as one.
May I offer you tea?

Soulful moan.

The air vibrates with a sound. Can you hear it? A moan, deep and raw, carried on the wind of a lost people, the soulful
sorrow of despair and pain. Misery of bearing the weight of two worlds; first, wearing the mask of indifference not to stir
fears and anxieties of the descendants of those who created this condition of living in a racially biased society.
Second, the mask of fear, which leads to to attempts of securing a space to become clear and weightless to experience
peace and liberation under the shadow of blackness.

The wailing rings in my soul, unlocking history of captive and captor, enslaved and master, consumer and owner. The
sweet sound gives me hope to be recognized and viewed as a human with emotions, talents, and spirituality. This moan allows my third eye to acknowledge the

unjust and the injustices that has been intertwined in
this society
throughout history.

Defiance, passion, and spirituality are the patriots of this moan. The everlasting moan of a lost village with no brotherhood with the land that birthed my ancestors rings loudly in my heart. We lament together sharing the sorrow and
pain that we only can bare. Can you hear it?

Listen.

The world whispers secrets, if you'll only listen. Laughter drips from rain clouds, the wind plays a forest's song, and the
waves dance with untamed joy. Amidst this symphony, a soul inhales, seeking the warmth of another. Can you hear the
gentle pulse of a loving heart's embrace?

Listen, and you can hear the shattering impact, the moment a life ends in the delusion of paradise. The promised virgins
are drowned out by the screams of mangled bodies, the hollow eyes of shell-shocked children. And beneath it all, the
terrified whispers of a crowd, butchered for the earth's riches, Sudan's lifeblood turned to death.

Listen. Can you hear the fractured cries, the desperate shouts of a mind adrift in a sea of pharmaceuticals? Meant to

calm, they instead create a tempest, a chemical storm
that ravages both body and soul.
Every moment reveals its truth, if you only listen.

Out of Africa: A Sapling in Exile.

Out of the rich earth of Africa, a new life takes root in unfamiliar ground. Though transplanted, its influence spreads through generations, leaving an indelible mark on everything it touches. This lineage, a tapestry woven from diverse origins and traditions, adapts and blends into its surroundings, sometimes concealed by the dominant landscape. Yet, this growth bears the scars of alien ideologies, the echoes of forced marches and distorted narratives, forever marked by the degradation of the vessel that carried it from its homeland. This tree, once part of a vast forest, was violently uprooted and transported.

Now, this African sapling navigates a world with foreign soil and minerals, yet it persists in its growth. The connection to its Ethiopian origin has been severed, the memory of its beginnings obscured and twisted. A yearning arises: Father Kibish, can I return to the sacred banks of the Blue Nile, immerse myself in the holy waters of Lake Tana? Can I taste the pure essence that once nourished you, hoping it will bring clarity to this clouded past? The truth of my beginnings is entangled in falsehoods, and I am but a young descendant, with limited understanding, led away from Africa into the shadows of colonial rule.

Out of Africa, my ancestors, standing tall, revealed to the world the innate brilliance of humankind, from the dawn of the Stone Age to the mastery of iron, while the early inhabitants of Europe lived in a more rudimentary state. In the ancient lands of Ethiopia, the original people bathed in pristine streams, moved in harmony with the rhythms of nature, forging a deep connection to the land, a vibrant unity that seemed to bridge the earthly and the divine. Now, thrust out of Africa and into the moral decay of the unknown, this resilient tree continues to grow, Bearing witness to a complex and painful inheritance.

The Oak Tree of the Ghetto.

Ghetto child, lost in this labyrinth we call life, feeling alien in a world that perceives you as a menace, a beast. You yearn for the solace of home, a sanctuary of security and embrace. A stranger's loving smile, offered as kindness, is met with suspicion in your guarded gaze – a perceived threat. Confusion clouds your mind, confronted by images that celebrate foolishness, figures stumbling through existence, striving for stardom but radiating only the dimness of a moonless night.

Ghetto child, root yourself deep, stand resilient as an oak tree against the brutal truths of this existence, this mental prison of twisted perceptions, born from impoverished conditions, on dirt paths worn smooth by generations. This mental prison is a cycle, a relentless rotation of disillusionment, frustration, and self-medication, ensuring the projects and wards remain perpetually full. Yet, you possess a sixth sense, a blessing that warns you of danger and contempt. Heed its call, fly away from energies intended to harm you.

Ghetto child, let your spirit ascend to the heavens of past kings and queens, your heritage. Soar with them and witness your own greatness, your inherent beauty. You descend from a majestic lineage, and therefore, you are a king, possessing a strength yet to be fully unleashed. Rise above despair, conquer this maze of life. Embody the living example for others to follow. Live, ghetto child, truly live.

The Divided Eden.

My Queen, my love for you is absolute, unwavering. There are no shortcuts on the path to you; you feel as distant and unknown as the universe itself. When I try to picture you, the images become warped, distorted like reflections in rippling
water, making your beauty appear misshapen and strange.

My Queen, the origin of all life, the Garden of Eden, has been torn apart, its pieces divided among nations devoid of true color, who greedily amass wealth while poverty and death shroud your children. I am deeply troubled. I see the deep wounds inflicted upon your body, wounds that breed division and cause a hemorrhage of your precious resources, fueling endless wars fought by expendable players. The land once flowing with abundance has become dust and blood.

You are the genesis, my protector in times of suffering, yet you exist only in my dreams. Dreams of finding solace in your sacred waters, of running freely in your Edenic gardens. I can hear your call, I can feel your essence, and my heart swells with pride knowing my humble beginnings lie with you. Queen, your spirit, dark and profound, burns within me, and you reign with patience and love, even if only within the realm of my dreams.

Fleeting Beauty.

Excuse me miss, my heart just stopped. Is your name perhaps... Stunning? Because the moment my eyes, these brown eyes, met the depths of your hazel gaze, I was utterly stunned. It was a brief yet profound glance, and in that instant, I felt I truly saw you. My soul trembled, and a sudden drop resonated within me.

Ms. Redbone, with a complexion of a Lay's potato chip, my mind erupted with visions of a future overflowing with unrestrained joy, a euphoric rhythm of two spirits becoming one. Ms. Red, you have taken over my dreams, breathed life into this very soul.

A stranger, yet you now occupy my thoughts, adding vibrant texture to my dreams of red roses, black suits, and white dresses. In my mind's eye, we dance in perfect harmony, our spirits swimming as a single entity. What fantasy have you possibly escaped? You move with the effortless grace of wind whispering through a forest, and your presence flows like wine being poured – both deliberate and breathtakingly swift. May I experience the warmth of your beauty and taste your liquid desire?

Ms. Red, with that small waist and those succulent hips, a backside that evokes images of Africa. Here I sit on this bus, completely absorbed by your beauty and captivated by the sweet sound of your reasonable voice. I am eager to know you, to understand your way of life. Show me yourself, so I can fully embrace your essence. You are the butterfly holding the answers to my many questions.

"Ding dong," the stop requested, my time is up. As the bus doors open, the butterfly departs. Though she leaves, I carry her with me in my memory, and I will not forget this bus ride with Ms. Red. Goodbye for now. Shit! I missed my stop.

Yearning in Thought.

Again, my love, I find myself adrift in thoughts of you. Whether sleeping or awake, I drift, my mind becoming as light as a cloud, filled with fantasies of our two energies merging, coalescing in a thunderous wave of bliss. I feel the elation of a lottery win, yet the frustration of a misplaced ticket, able only to touch you in my thoughts, not in reality.

To be so close to having all I desire, with you being that very desire. You inspire great deeds in ordinary souls. I envision a future brimming with peace and togetherness, our beings melting together to create a vision of love and happiness. My love, do not fret; destiny itself forged our union, igniting this energy within me. Know this: a circle begins at one point and inevitably reconnects at that same point, an unbreakable bond.

I continue to drift on thoughts of you.

Forbidden Fantasy.

Behold me, this creature of deep, burnished wood, a living testament to ages past. You desire to master me, to wield this ancient armor that gleams like the moonlit night. You gaze upon me, your soul a battleground of wonder and dread. You ponder the sensation of this embrace, yearning for the warmth of my essence to permeate your being, to ignite a sense of profound unity.

Let the weight of my reality fill your mind, the fear I inspire transforming into a primal aversion. Yet, your curiosity, a relentless adversary, fans the flames of forbidden fantasy. I return to your thoughts, piercing your soul, stirring emotions into a tempest of unsettling bliss, teetering on the edge of madness. To awaken dormant sensations, feel the surge of my energy, a spear that compels your mind to surrender to this alien wonder.

Dispel the haze of excitement, and feel the raw intensity

as I delve deeper, planting the seed of my essence within your core. Look at me, for I see you, too.

Echoes of Brotherhood.

Say something! I see my reflection, a figure hesitant, held back by fear from acting on the heart's deepest desires. I yearn for a brotherly embrace, a shared connection with you. If only a glance, a subtle nod, could bridge the distance, allowing our minds to intertwine, our hearts to beat in the resonant rhythm of ancestral drums, a sacred union.

My brother, with our spirits joined, we could ascend to realms of profound understanding, drinking from the well of our ancestors' wisdom. Forgive my past blindness, the haze of doubt and misguided notions that clouded my perception. Our connection is under siege, bombarded by whispers of envy and greed, attempting to sever the bond.

Let us close our eyes and ears to these distractions, and open the inner eye of reason, seeking to overstand each other's needs, to embrace the unique path each of us walks. Let us savor the richness of each other's experiences, exchanging knowledge like sacred offerings, until we are both overflowing with wisdom. Two mystical forces, like thunder and lightning, shaping the very world around us. Our shared history binds our spirits, and I carry my brothers within my heart, radiating unity and love for all to witness.

"I have spoken."

The Dance of Release.

I crave the unfamiliar, a warmth that burns with a different fire, a stranger whose hidden depths hold a treasure beyond price, a treasure I yearn to possess, to hold captive. Call me the insider, the one who seeks the forbidden. A loneliness echoes in my voice, a hunger for the strange. I desire the verbal dance that ignites my senses, that awakens the core of my being. I long for a seductive interplay of expressions, a visual symphony of positions that rival the Kama Sutra. Speak to me in the hues of rose, earth, and moonlight.

My senses are heightened, and I detect the ringless fingers, the souls searching for a bond, for a lost connection. The faded tan lines, the marks of past commitments, speak of a yearning for what was, or what might have been. They seek connection through the language of the body, a love born of desire. The intricate designs etched across their skin, revealed in the moon's glow, tell stories of their journeys.

I crave the strange, the thrilling, the irresistible. My energy is focused, my intent sharp. My smile, a devilish invitation, amplifies the desire within. I seek to lose myself in the depths of shared passion. I relish this complex dance, the way my words can stir emotions, awaken curiosity. The physical response to my playful pursuit, the teasing of the mind that culminates in release. Through the language of sighs, moans, and intertwined forms, my hunger is satiated.

Jasmine.

'Daddy, you're so silly!' And yes, I am, my love, because you fill my world with joy, and my heart beats solely for you. You've given me life anew and I'm eternally grateful that a part of me lives within you. The silliness you inspire is a unique and precious gift, my seed of joy. Your beauty and talent dazzle my soul, lifting my spirit to heavenly realms where I bathe in boundless love. My beautiful child, your grace has bestowed upon me a pride that towers above Mount Everest.

It was love at first sight when I gazed upon you, my angel, my gift. My silliness, as clear as a dark bean in milky white, is a testament to my boundless love. A silly father, utterly devoted to the spirit that has nourished my soul and granted me everlasting love. Your face is a reflection of mine, and in you, I see my dreams made real. Yes, I am silly, proud as a peacock displaying vibrant feathers that shimmer like starlight. You've given me riches beyond measure, an immeasurable wealth of love. Your smile touches my heart, and tears of joy, like rain released from a dark cloud, wash over me. You transform my madness into a warmth that fills my being and strengthens my love for you. Stand back, my love, and witness your silly father and his undying devotion.

Forging Understanding.

I search, I seek you, my heart a thunderous charge, like elephants in a frenzied stampede, anticipating the moment of capture. My soul, programmed to embrace the beautiful divergence of human beings, continues its quest. To be freed, to explore the boundless dimensions of consciousness, to forge vessels of understanding, and shatter the chains of pre-packaged knowledge that hold our minds captive. Where, oh where, must I look?

This search, an inheritance passed down through generations, like worn clothes from cousin to cousin, or unpaid debts accumulating interest, growing monstrous with each transfer. In vain, it seems, this search persists, winding and weaving like the mighty Mississippi, a river of longing, ever flowing, ever living.

Forgive me, my mind has not yet forged the strength to reach its furthest bounds, in pursuit of you. Nonetheless, the search continues.

Echoes of the Ancestors: A Mystic's Lament and Invocation.

Oh, ancient echoes, spirits woven into the fabric of my being, I summon you! A tempest rages within, a shadow play of existence that shatters the fragile sanctuary of my soul. The veils of reality shimmer. And chaos, a hungry specter, dances unchecked.

My inner sanctum, once a still pool, now churns with turbulent currents. I stumble, a vessel adrift, lost in the labyrinth of fleeting illusions. I beseech you, ancestral luminaries, bathe me in the celestial glow of Chandra, the moon's serene radiance. Illuminate the hidden pathways, guide my feet upon the sacred thread of righteousness, and bestow upon me the balm of profound peace.

Forgive my frailties, for I am but a fledgling, a child lost in the bewildering expanse of existence. The whispers of deceit, spun from ethereal threads, ensnare my senses. I am a clumsy marionette, my spirit a wanderer in a realm unseen, while my form remains tethered to this earthly plane.

Ancestors, the sacred dance of Sancharyoga, the ancient wisdom passed through generations, has faded, its rhythm lost in the mists of time. I am a vessel emptied of its sacred contents. I implore you, bestow upon me the fortitude to withstand the storm, to defy the encroaching shadows of chaos and confusion.

The world presents itself as a two-sided mirror, reflecting a distorted reality, a phantasm of fairness and justice, while I endure the sting of relentless denial. I am hunted by a phantom, a needle-sharp presence crafted to pierce the very essence of my being.

Yet, from the depths of your ethereal realm, I feel your strength coursing through me, a primal energy awakening within. You ignite the fire of resilience, the spirit to stand defiant against the cold indifference and the gaping maw of injustice. Hear my fervent cry, oh ancestral guardians, and grant me the mystical fortitude to endure, to transcend, and to reclaim the serenity that is my birthright.

Tides of Disillusionment: A Chronicle of Eroding Faith.

The tides of time have eroded my faith in humanity, revealing the jagged scars of self-deception. My conscience, a weary sentinel, whispers warnings of imagined notions, of perceptions twisted into weapons. Selfless ambitions, cloaked in shadows, birth a harvest of pain and terror, sowing discord across cultures, generations, and seasons, all for the fleeting allure of wealth and power.

Deeds of avarice, wrought by those who masquerade as corporations, merchants of minerals, their hands stained with genocide and manipulation, their bellies swollen with the spoils of nations. Without faith, hope withers, and the sun, weary of witnessing our darkness, closes its eye, denying us the comfort of its warmth.

People starve, while the greedy feast on ill-gotten gains, harvested from the bones of the exploited. Empathy, the very essence of our humanity, evaporates like steam, leaving behind a chilling void. Greed, a ravenous beast, consumes all, leaving only the hollow echo of gluttony. Faith drained to an empty abyss, only the venom of hate can fill the void, a chilling testament to our collective descent.

Ocean's Lush Rhythm.

Let me ride the surging tide of your ocean, feel the push and pull of your intimate rhythm. This boundless ocean of yours, I yearn to plunge into its deepest trenches, seeking the hidden pearl that is you. Let me taste the slick sweetness of your peach, let its plumpness envelop me, its juice a warm flood against my skin. You brush past, a tantalizing wave of womanly grace, your scent a heady brew that ignites a primal hunger. Let that juice spill onto my tongue, let its intoxicating warmth spread through me, leaving me deliciously undone.

I sway on the precipice, unbalanced by the intoxicating rhythm of your waves, those luscious mounds that beckon. Inside your ocean's embrace, a tremor starts, a tingling that builds like a volcano about to burst, hot lava desire spilling through my veins. This ocean of yours, so powerfully sensual, yet capable of a breathtaking tenderness, like a soft breeze whispering across a ripe peach, a single drop of dew tracing its sweet curve. You are a taste I crave, a sweetness that lingers.

The Unsettled Self.

The skin whispers Africa, but the spirit roars a warrior's cry. Inside, a battle rages between the roots that clutch this soil and the phantom echoes of a distant home. I walk this land, familiar yet alien, where my ancestors were broken and bound. Once, in dreams, I wore a crown, led kin of intellect, spoke with spirits both bright and shadowed, and knew kinship with the swift hare and the mighty lion.

Who am I now? Born of an Black American mother, skin kissed by the African sun of my father, I am a paradox in a nation that both covets and fears the very essence of me. Am I African American? Black? African? The labels blur, a confusing shroud. In the realm of sleep, I am unburdened, splashing in warm currents, running free across the Serengeti with brothers whose skin mirrors mine. I dream of a power that mends and heals, a shaman's touch lost to waking hours.
This life unfolds with a sense of déjà vu, a path trod by many before me, many yet to come. The humid breath of

the African jungle nourishes my flesh and soul, yet the tongue of my ancestors remains a mystery, a lost key to my truest self. I have learned the venomous language of hate and fear, the cunning ways of those who amassed fortunes from stolen labor and stolen lives. Entertainment and sport now serve as pacifiers for their descendants.

Who am I? A slave of the past, perhaps still a slave in a different guise, mistaking movement for true progress. Only evolution marches forward, and I scramble to keep pace. I am an African on foreign soil, yearning for a homeland my eyes have never seen, a place of untamed beauty and sweet abundance, a motherland robbed of millions of her children.

I am an African diluted by names and lies, blindfolded in a world that demands success while denying true belonging. An African whose very being reflects the enduring love of those who came before. I am an African confused and wounded, seeking a truth that has been obscured. That is who I am.

A Cry for Sudan.

The specter of escalating violence looms over Sudan. Forces are mobilizing, and the cries of my brothers and sisters echo with fear. The land of our ancestors trembles as millions face the agonizing choice: flee to unfamiliar lands or risk the unimaginable. Blood stains the earth, a grim tide threatening to engulf our nation. My heart aches, and my spirit shatters with each report of brutality.

Sudan is facing its darkest hour. Innocent lives are being extinguished – babies starved, homes reduced to ash, girls violated and scarred, religious identities erased. The echoes of past horrors resonate with chilling familiarity. Marauders descend, leaving behind a trail of destruction and death. Where is the justice? The silence of the world is deafening.

To my dear Sudanese people: Your survival demands immediate action. Run. Your life hangs in the balance. This land, now stained with terror, empties the soul and shakes the spirit. Do not succumb to despair. Do not suffer the fate of Rwanda or the tyranny of Idi Amin. Run, though the shadows of violence pursue you, fueled by fear and the scent of blood. Do not look back; seek safety with every fiber of your being.

To the international community: The time for passive observation is over. The atrocities unfolding in Sudan demand immediate and decisive intervention. We implore you!

Demand an immediate cessation of hostilities.

Provide safe passage and humanitarian aid to those fleeing.

Hold the perpetrators of violence accountable for their crimes.

Stand in solidarity with the people of Sudan in their hour of need.

Let the cries from Sudan not fall on deaf ears. Let compassion and a commitment to justice guide our actions. Let hope be the beacon that leads Sudan out of this abyss.

Fortified by Spirit, Illuminated by Truth: A Tribute to My Ancestors.

The echoes of my cries reached my ancestors, and they felt my pain. Now, I have claimed my worries and set them aside. I give thanks to the highest. My ancestors, your blessing is the spirit that fortifies my soul, a constant light that has never dimmed on this uncertain path.

Pride once stood as a shield before my inner eye, obscuring truth. Yet, ancestors, your divine grace has enveloped my stumbles, granting me the awareness to see the strength and security in the love and support offered to my vulnerable spirit. Thank you, my lords; my third eye now opens to the boundless panorama of life's wonders. My left side holds a powerful strength, for which I offer everlasting praise.

My ancestors, I sing your praises. The heavy yoke has

been lifted from my mind, and I walk upright in all that I am. What a sweet relief to be free from doubt, as sorrows recede, confusion fades, and a clear sky of understanding dawns within me. Praises to my ancestors.